WORLD FACTS

Written by Fiona Waters

Illustrated by Robin Edmonds

HENDERSON
PUBLISHING LTD

THE EARTH – OUR HOME

The Earth is one of nine planets circling the Sun. Together they are called the *solar system*. Our nearest neighbour is Venus – which is a mere 40 million km (25 million miles) away!

We think the Earth is ginormous, but it is actually quite small compared to some of the other planets. It whirls around in space at 80,000 kph (50,000 mph).

1 *Mercury*
2 *Venus*
3 *Earth*
4 *Mars*
5 *Jupiter*
6 *Saturn*
7 *Uranus*
8 *Neptune*
9 *Pluto*

HOLIDAY SNAPS

Pictures of Earth taken from space show a wonderful blue globe in the darkness, with only a red glow from the Sun and the odd pale twinkle of the stars.

The Earth photographed by Apollo astronauts returning from the Moon

Our Big Little Earth

The distance from the North Pole to the South Pole is 12,714 km (7,900 miles) and the diameter of the Earth around the equator is 12,758 km (7,927 miles).

Flat World?

Many early civilizations believed that the world was flat. The Hindus thought that it was a plate balanced on the backs of four elephants who were standing on a turtle! Eh?

Big Electricity Bill?

The Sun gives the Earth light and heat, and will continue to do so for another staggering five billion years into the future!

What the Earth's Made of

The Earth has four layers – a crust (nothing to do with a loaf of bread!), a mantle and an outer and inner core.

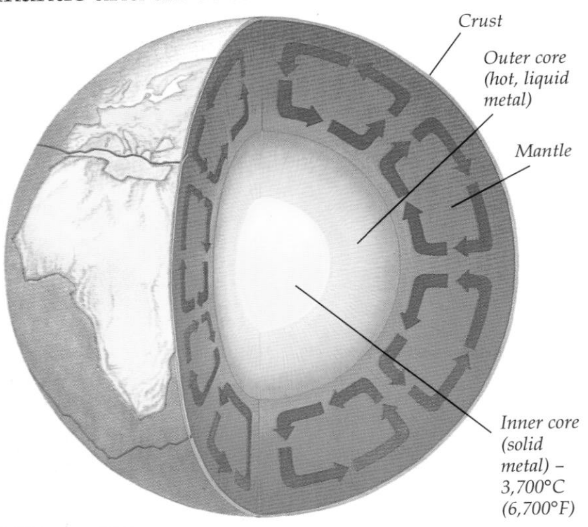

Water, Water Everywhere!

Over two-thirds of the Earth's surface is covered by water. The picture shown here is a view of the Pacific Ocean from a satellite. It seems to cover most of the Earth.

Believe It or Not...

All the Earth's land could fit in the Pacific Ocean. Wow!

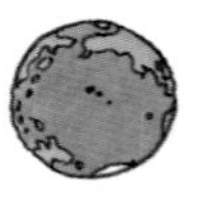

On the Move

Most of the Earth's water is in the ocean. The rest is fresh water in rivers and lakes, ground water (rain which soaks into the soil) and the moisture in the atmosphere (the envelope of air around the Earth).

The Water Cycle

Not a strange ocean-going bicycle, but the continual, circular journey of water from the sky, to the ground and up to the sky again. Here's how it works:

1. Sun heats oceans, lakes and land.

2. Heated water on land turns into invisible water vapour and rises into sky. (This is evaporation.)

3. Water collects as droplets, forming clouds.

4. Big droplets fall as rain.

5. Rain falls back to land to begin the journey again.

Great Atmosphere!

The Earth's atmosphere is quite unlike that of the other planets, and is made from the gases originally given out by volcanoes. 78% is nitrogen and the rest is mostly oxygen with tiny amounts of argon and neon.

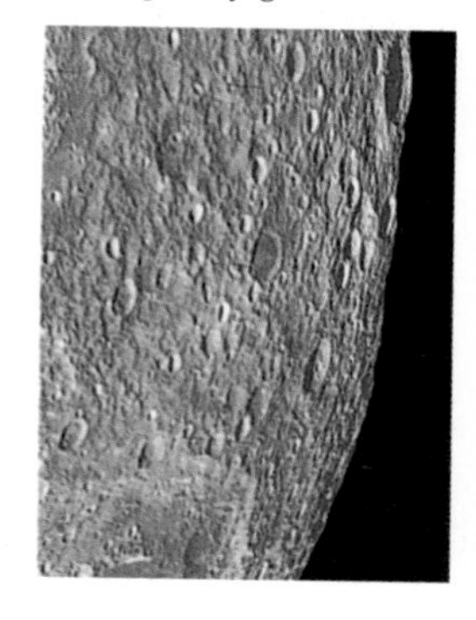

Dry and Dark

The Moon orbits the Earth. (It is a satellite, not a planet.) It has no atmosphere and no weather, and the sky is always black. Maybe not the ideal holiday destination!

ROCK ON!

The Earth's surface is made up of three basic types of rock.

Igneous – these were the first rocks ever, formed as the Earth began to cool

Sedimentary – these rocks are formed out of the bits and pieces of weathered rocks that became squashed in layers at the bottom of rivers and oceans

Metamorphic – these are igneous or sedimentary rocks that have been changed either by pressure or heat

HARD-WEARING

The most common igneous rock is granite. It is often used to build houses as it is very strong and tough, and can withstand bad weather.

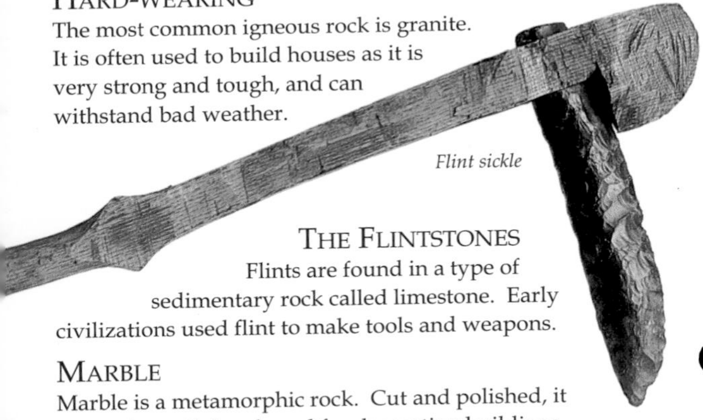

Flint sickle

THE FLINTSTONES

Flints are found in a type of sedimentary rock called limestone. Early civilizations used flint to make tools and weapons.

MARBLE

Marble is a metamorphic rock. Cut and polished, it is very beautiful and used for decorating buildings and sculpture.

Taj Mahal

Detail of marble inlay work on the Taj Mahal

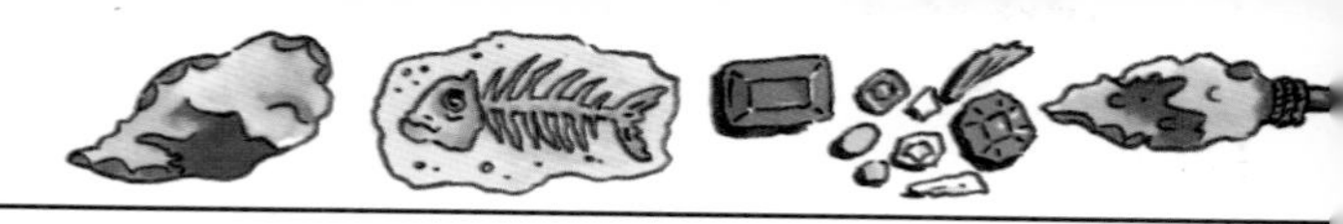

Marvellous Minerals

All rocks are made up of elements called minerals. A look at a piece of granite through a strong microscope reveals all the minerals looking quite spectacular!

Crystal Clear

Many minerals form regular shapes called crystals. For many years, people thought that crystals were ice.

Natural crystals can look very beautiful and are cut to make gemstones such as diamonds, rubies and emeralds.

These magnificent crystals have formed from hot watery solutions within the Earth.

Aquamarine

Pink morganite

Greenish heliodor

Yellow heliodor

Cut heliodor

Cut aquamarine

Fossil Remains

Fossils are the remains of animals or plants that died long ago and have gradually turned into stone.

This fossil lobster is about 80 million years old!

THE CONTINENTAL DRIFT

The continents are the seven enormous land masses that make up the Earth's land surface. If you were to cut their shapes out of your atlas, you would discover a very curious thing – the continents fit fairly closely together, give or take a few gaps!

A CLOSER FIT

Scientists have discovered that 250 million years ago, the continents were probably joined as one huge land mass. They named it *Pangaea*.

A VAST CONTINENT

The biggest continent is Asia, with an area of 44,485,900 sq km (17,176,090 sq miles). That's REALLY big! In fact, both Europe and Africa would fit into Asia with room to spare.

International Crawler

The common garden snail can be found in the British Isles and in the eastern USA. As this would be too far for it to have swum (even if it could!), its early ancestors must have crawled from one place to another when the land was one piece.

Common garden snails

Believe It or Not...

The continents are still on the move – only a few centimetres a year, but the movement can be measured. Yikes!

America and Europe drift away from each other by about 4 cm (1.6 in), and the Rift Valley in Africa gets 1 mm wider every year.

THE VIOLENT EARTH

Earthquakes are caused by the movement of the giant plates that make up the Earth's crust. In some places, plates slide under each other gradually, but in others they push and push against each other, until one plate suddenly slips over the other. This makes shock waves which we feel as an earthquake.

THE RICHTER SCALE

The Richter Scale is used to record the amount of energy released by an earthquake. Scientific instruments pick up about 500,000 earthquakes a year. Most are so small they barely measure on the Richter Scale, but about 1,000 each year are newsworthy.

THE MERCALLI SCALE

The Mercalli Scale is a scale of 1 to 12 which grades earthquakes by observing their effects. For example, 3 = hanging light bulbs swing; 6 = movements felt, pictures fall off walls and windows break; 12 = almost total destruction.

Believe It or Not...

Earthquakes usually last less than a minute.

Toads and Dragons

The first instrument for measuring earthquakes was invented in China in AD 132. When there was an earthquake, the bronze balls in the dragons' mouths would drop into the mouths of the toads below. Nifty, eh!

Zhang Heng's seismoscope

Early Warnings

Animals seem to sense when there is going to be an earthquake. Dogs howl, rats leave their holes and horses get restless. Not surprising, really!

Moonquakes

The Moon has quakes, but they are usually caused by meteorites (rock-like objects from space).

ERUPTION

Volcanoes often lie dormant (quiet and inactive) for hundreds of years, but beware once they become active! They can shoot ash, rocks and gas miles up into the atmosphere, and it becomes as dark as night. People are killed or left homeless and crops are destroyed.

Mount Etna is one of the highest mountains and most active volcanoes in Europe.

FIRE DOWN BELOW

If you were to journey to the centre of the Earth, you would get pretty hot! 200 km (120 miles) in, the temperature is 1,500°C (2,732°F) but you need to go even deeper before the rocks melt and become *molten* (liquid). If the molten rock, called *magma*, manages to reach the surface as the Earth's plates shift, it bursts out and is called *lava*.

PANIC IN THE STREETS

Mount Vesuvius, in Italy, is famous for its eruption in AD 79, which buried the towns of Pompeii and Herculaneum.

Over 2,000 people died in Pompeii as the hot ash poured down on to the town. It all happened so quickly that their remains seem to have been frozen in time, at the moment of death.

Believe It or Not...

The loaf of bread shown here was freshly baked – 2,000 years ago! You can still see the baker's stamp.

Remains Revealed

The ash that fell from Vesuvius set round the bodies of the unfortunate people and animals who could not get away. The bodies decayed with time, but their shapes were left in the hardened ash. The hollows can be filled with plaster and the tragic victims revealed.

This mother is trying to protect her child.

Storm Clouds Ahead

Storm clouds gathering in the sky can mean that serious weather is on the way.

Thunder and Lightning

Claps of thunder and streaks of lightning can be very frightening – especially if you are outside! Lightning always goes for tall, isolated objects, so never shelter under a tree in a storm.

Near or Far?

To work out how far away a storm is, count the number of seconds after seeing the lightning, until you hear the thunder. For every 2 seconds, the storm is a kilometre away.

Believe It or Not...

US park ranger Roy Sullivan was struck by lightning seven times in thirty five years! How unlucky can you get!

What's in a Name?

Hurricanes, typhoons and cyclones are all the same thing – they are called hurricanes in the Atlantic, cyclones in the Indian Ocean and typhoons in the Pacific!

At full blow, a hurricane wind will blow at 360 kph (220 mph) and cause absolute devastation.

Eye Eye!

A great many hurricanes build up over the ocean, which is where the photograph shown here was taken. You can see the 'eye' at the centre of the storm quite clearly.

I Name This Hurricane...

Names have been given to all hurricanes since 1954. Until the 1970s female names were used, but now male/female names are used alternately!

Tornadoes, Twisters and Whirlwinds

Tornadoes, twisters and whirlwinds are here one moment and gone the next, leaving a trail of destruction behind.

A tornado can pick things up, send them high into the sky and then put them down quite unharmed hundreds of metres away! Incredible!

The World's Oceans

Over two-thirds of the Earth's surface is under water. The five oceans make up most of this. They are the Pacific, Atlantic, Indian, Southern and Arctic.

Grains of Sand

Waves crashing on to the shore can exert a pressure of 25 tonnes per square metre. A human foot landing on the ground exerts a pressure thirty times less! This constant pounding is what reduces huge stones to the finest sand.

Making Waves

Waves have been recorded travelling at about 900 kph (559 mph). That's much faster than the world water speed record of 556 kph (345 mph), achieved by a hydroplane.

The highest wave was estimated to be 85 m (278 ft) high – almost the same height as the Statue of Liberty in New York.

Sea Mountains

Underwater landscapes look remarkably similar to that above! There are mountains, valleys, ridges and plains. The highest underwater mountain is 8,705 m (28,560 ft), compared to Mount Everest, the highest land mountain, which is 8,848 m (29,028 ft).

Ocean Harvests

70 million tonnes of fish are caught every year, as well as lobsters, shrimps, clams, crabs, squid and mussels. The sea gives us other useful products such as salt, sponges and beautiful pearls. Deeper down, the ocean floor yields diamonds, coal, oil, gas, sand and gravel.

Believe It or Not...

- There is more gold dissolved in sea water than there is to be found on land!

- The total amount of salt in the world's oceans and seas would cover the whole of Europe to a depth of 5 km (3 miles)!

SURROUNDED BY WATER

Some islands are so big they don't feel like islands! Greenland, the world's largest island, is 2,175,219 sq km (839,852 sq miles) across. Alongside that, Great Britain is quite small at 218,065 sq km (84,195 sq miles).

I WANT TO BE ALONE

The world's most remote island is Bouvet Island,which is about 1,700 km (1,056 miles) from its nearest neighbour, Queen Maud Land on the coast of eastern Antarctica.

HIGH TIDE ISLANDS

Each time the tide comes in, some pieces of mainland get cut off by water and become short-term islands, like Mont St Michel in France, for instance.

Mont St Michel is only an island at high tide.

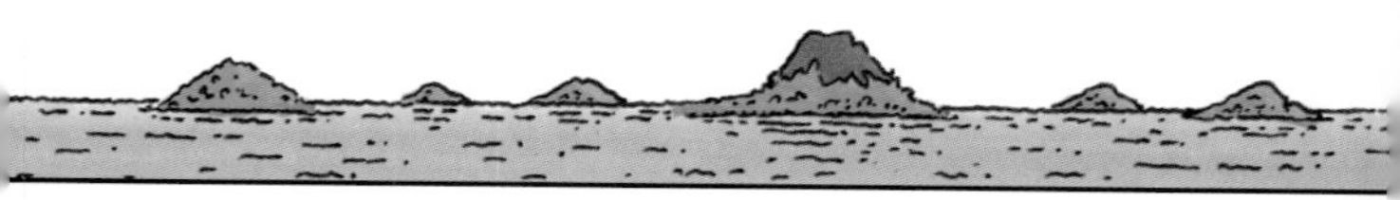

Volcanic Islands

Some islands in Hawaii are actually the tops of volcanoes. When lava poured out of the volcano Kilauea in the 1980s, it flowed down into the sea and made new land.

Like icebergs, volcanic islands have more hidden below the sea than above. Kilauea is actually the tallest mountain on earth (from sea floor to summit) at 10,000 m (32,800 ft).

Thousands of Islands

Japan is made up of a chain of about 3,900 volcanic islands, but Indonesia has the world's biggest island chain. It has a staggering 17,000 islands which go through three time zones!

River Deep...

Most of the Earth's fresh water is frozen as ice or trapped in rocks. Less than one percent is contained in the world's rivers and lakes. Amazing!

This map shows the largest lakes and rivers in the world, marked in blue. The largest lake, the Caspian Sea, would almost cover Japan, and the longest river, the Nile, could reach from Berlin to New York!

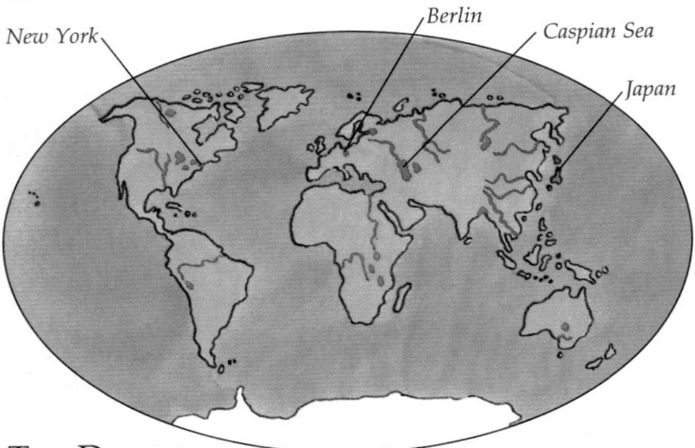

The Deepest...

The deepest lake is Lake Baikal in Siberia. At 162 m (5,315 ft) it would cover five Eiffel Towers standing on top of each other!

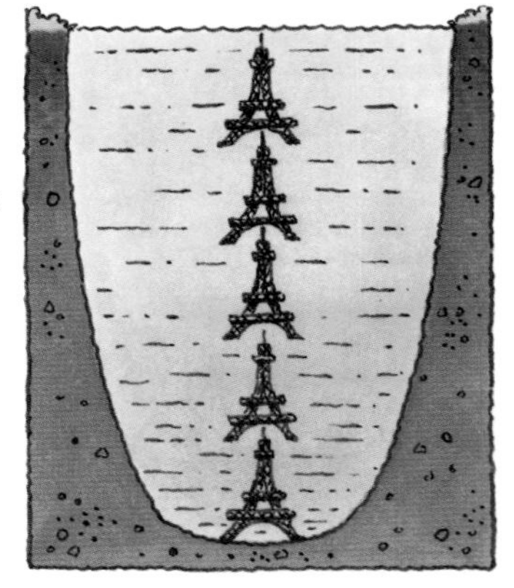

The Longest...

The longest river in the world is the Nile in Africa – 6,695 km (4,160 miles) from start to finish!

Trickle to Torrent

About 180,000 cubic metres (6.4 million cubic feet) of water flows out of the Amazon into the ocean every second. It would take just over a second to fill London's St Paul's Cathedral!

Dry Rivers?

Some rivers hardly ever have any water in them!

The Todd River in central Australia usually looks like this:

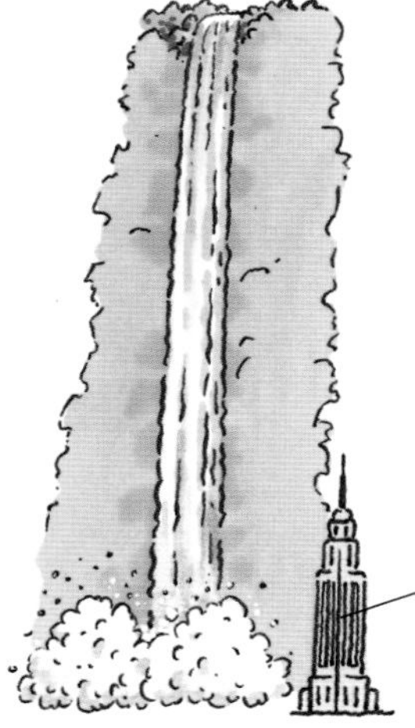

Empire State Building

The Highest...

The highest waterfall in the world is in Venezuela. The total drop of the Angel Falls, at 979 m (3,212 ft) is almost three times as high as the Empire State Building! The falls take their name from the American pilot Jimmy Angel, who found them in 1935.

...And Mountain High

The biggest mountain ranges in the world are made when the Earth's plates crash together, pushing the crust up into huge folds. Many mountains are still growing, and some of the oldest are slowly wearing away!

Young and Old

The 'young' mountains, like the Himalayas, were formed during the last few million years. 'Middle-aged' mountains, like the Urals, are decreasing in size, because they are gradually *eroded* (worn away). The REALLY old ones are so eroded that only a few low lying hills are left.

Believe It or Not...

The ten highest mountains in the world are all in the Himalayas.

All Change

The mountains that are volcanoes can change in appearance quite dramatically. Mount St Helens in the USA used to look like this (right).

It erupted in 1980 and now it looks like this (left)!

Mountaineers

In 1953, Edmund Hillary and Tenzing Norgay became the first people to climb Mount Everest, the world's highest mountain.

Top to Toe

Mountains are so high that the animal and plant life changes the further up you go! It's so cold at the top that nothing can survive, including human climbers who have to wear special equipment to breathe, see and keep warm.

Avalanche!

When snow and ice accumulate and then crash down the mountainside, it is called an *avalanche*. Avalanches can be very dangerous and can sweep away buildings or anything standing in the way.

Freshly fallen snow is full of air, so people who get buried can sometimes survive. Dogs are used to locate people buried beneath the surface.

Earthquake shaking may trigger avalanches that were just waiting to happen.

WATER FEATURES

Water (frozen and liquid), is responsible for carving out much of the world's landscape.

GLACIERS

A glacier is a thick mass of ice that begins high up in the mountains and moves downhill at the rate of about 2 m (6 ft) a day. It can take thousands of years for the ice in a slow-moving glacier to reach the bottom of a valley.

THE ICEMAN

In 1991, two climbers found a body frozen at the top of a glacier in a remote part of the Alps. Using radiocarbon dating, scientists decided that the body, known as the Iceman, had died somewhere between 3,350-3,300BC, which made him the oldest mummy in the world!

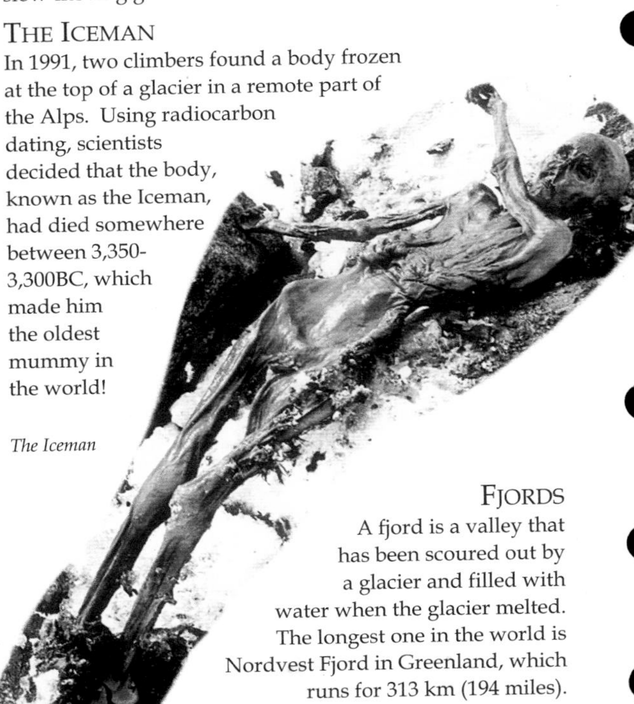

The Iceman

FJORDS

A fjord is a valley that has been scoured out by a glacier and filled with water when the glacier melted. The longest one in the world is Nordvest Fjord in Greenland, which runs for 313 km (194 miles).

The Grandest of All!

A canyon is a deep gorge carved through rock. The Grand Canyon, USA, is the largest gorge in the world. It is 349 km (217 miles) long and 1,676 m (5,499 ft) deep.

Believe It or Not...

The tallest stalagmite in the world is 32 m (105 ft) tall. The longest stalactite in the world is 6.2 m (20 ft 4 in) long.

Stalagmites and Stalactites

Limestone caves are hollowed out of the rocks over hundreds and hundreds of years. Stalagmites (which grow up) and stalactites (which grow down) are formed as the lime-filled water drips from the roof.

'HERE IS THE WEATHER...'

People have been forecasting the weather for very many years. Today's modern methods are probably a little more reliable than the old-fashioned ones, though.

THE OLD WAY

People used to rely on natural signs to predict the weather to come in the next few days.

In fact, there is little evidence to support any of these claims! However, some natural forecasting IS accurate. Pine cones will open in dry weather and close in wet, and seaweed hung by the door will harden in dry weather but become damp again if rain is coming.

'Red sky in the morning, shepherd's warning.'

'Red sky at night, shepherd's delight.'

Seaweed

Pine cones

Depression Ahead

24 hours a day, 7 days a week, all year round, sophisticated equipment monitors the weather. Satellites, balloons, radar, weather ships and weather stations collect weather facts. These are fed into powerful computers which produce forecasts.

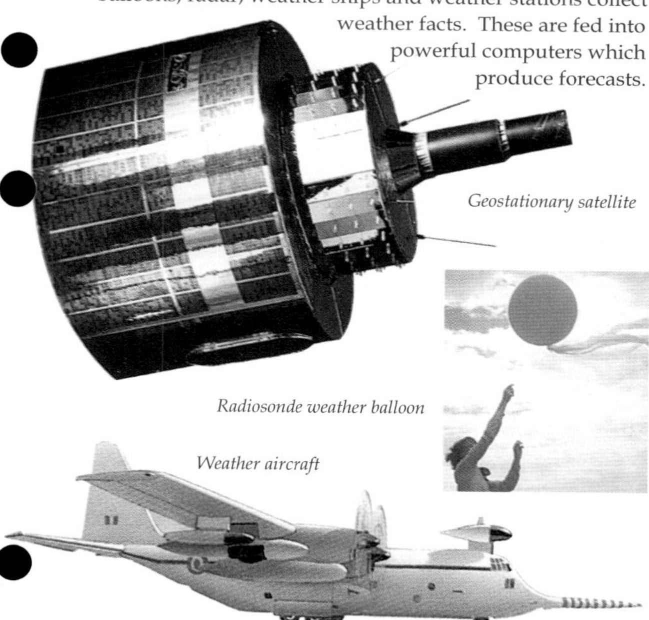

Geostationary satellite

Radiosonde weather balloon

Weather aircraft

Global View

Climate is a long-established pattern of weather for a particular area.

- At the Equator the temperature is about 25-30°C (77-86°F) every day. Phew!
- At the South Pole the average temperature is about -50°C (-122°F). (Your freezer is about -18°C (0°F).) Brrrrr!
- The Atacama Desert, Chile, has an average rainfall of only 0.51 mm (0.02 in) a year. Gasp!

Weather Features

Here are some extra snippets of weather info that you really shouldn't be without!

Cloudy Days

Clouds are all shapes, sizes and colours. In 1803, Englishman Luke Howard devised a system for classifying them. It was so simple that no one has been able to improve on it. He identified three basic types on which all other variations are based:

Puffy cumulus cloud

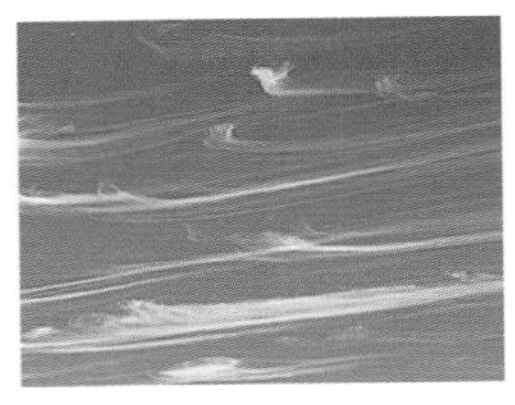

Feathery cirrus cloud

Layered stratus cloud

Wet, Wet, Wet...

The wettest place in the world is a mountain in Hawaii where over 11 m (approx. 35 ft) of rain falls every year. Squelch!

Weather Vanes

Weather vanes are probably one of the oldest weather-measuring instruments around. They swing around in the wind to show which direction it is blowing from.

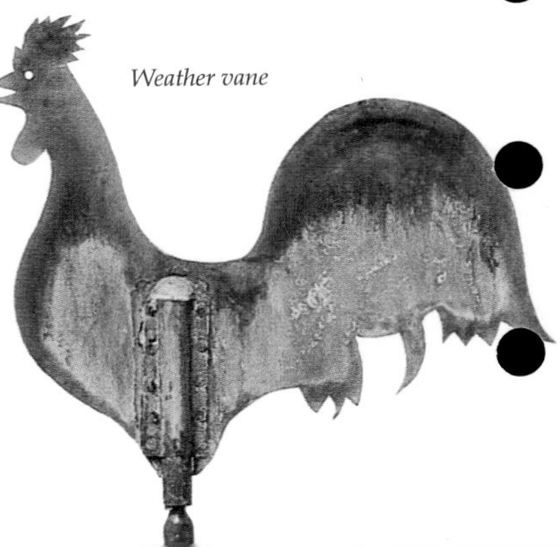

Weather vane

Believe It or Not...

All snowflakes have six sides, but photographed under a microscope no two have the same design.

Mountain Bloomers

Tiny flowers can survive in the mountains above the snowline. Called *alpines*, they burst into bloom as soon as the snow melts.

Rainbow Colours

The colours of a rainbow are always in the same order – red, orange, yellow, green, blue, indigo and violet!

Tree Trivia

There are many areas of the world where trees just cannot grow. They need at least 20 cm (7.9 in) of rain every year and a temperature of at least 10°C (50°F) in the summer to survive.

Redwood tree

Extraordinary Tree Facts

Tallest The tallest living tree is the same height as an Apollo space rocket – 111.25 m (365 ft) tall.

Oldest A bristlecone pine growing in Nevada, USA, is estimated to be 6,000 years old!

Widest Californian redwoods grow up to 7.6 m (25 ft) across! That's some trunk!

Heavy One cubic metre (1.3 cubic yards) of dried ebony weighs 1,030 kg (2,271 lb). The same volume of balsa weighs a mere 160 kg (234 lb).

Extra Large

It isn't just trees that can be ginormous! *Catalpas* or *Indian bean trees* have leaves 30 cm (1 ft) in length! Sugar pine cones have reached 65 cm (2 ft). A single cone can weigh as much as 500 g (1.1 lb).

WEIRD!

Swamp cypresses are seriously weird-looking trees. Their knobbly roots grow above the ground to collect oxygen, to help them survive and grow.

The swamp cypress flourishes in the bayou country of the southern United States. It is a deciduous conifer.

FORCEFUL

Trees can be amazingly strong! Their roots can break up buildings which grow nearby.

This tree in Cambodia is gradually breaking up the old temple wall on which it grows.

Weird Plants

Our world is home to some extraordinary plants. Beware though – don't get too close to some of them!

A Deadly Trap

Some plants are *carnivorous* (meat-eating) and live off insects and small animals. The venus flytrap actually closes its 'mouth' around an insect and starts to digest it within half an hour.

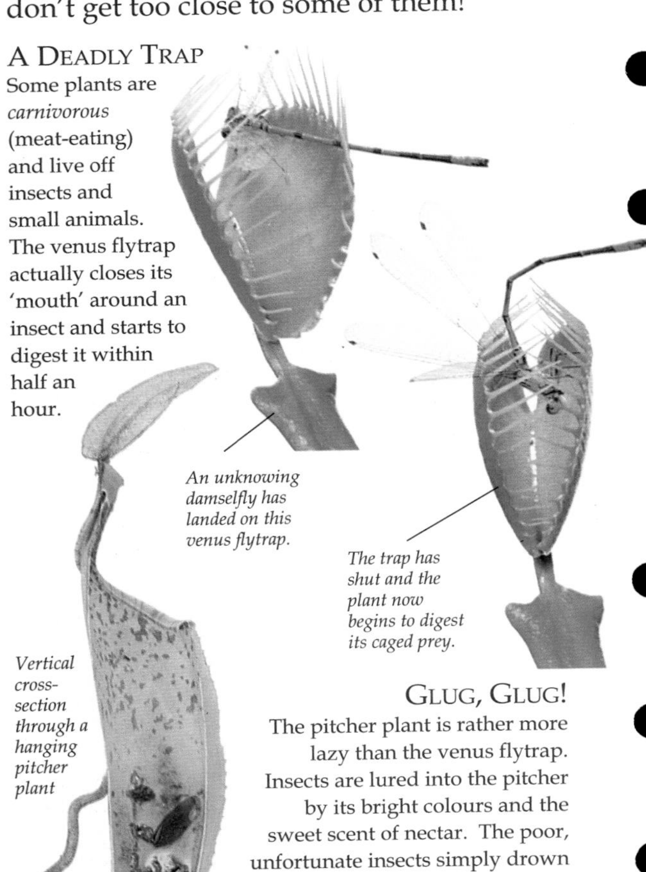

An unknowing damselfly has landed on this venus flytrap.

The trap has shut and the plant now begins to digest its caged prey.

Vertical cross-section through a hanging pitcher plant

Glug, Glug!

The pitcher plant is rather more lazy than the venus flytrap. Insects are lured into the pitcher by its bright colours and the sweet scent of nectar. The poor, unfortunate insects simply drown in the fluid at the bottom. Yuck!

What a Stinker!

Another real horror is the rafflesia plant. This nasty piece of work is huge. Each flower is about 1 m (3 ft) in diameter and weighs in at 7 kg (15 lb). Not content with being so vast, it is the smelliest plant ever. It has a putrid smell, like rotten meat. Pooo-eee!

Bean and Gone?

Watch out for the bean of the castor oil plant! Its poison is so powerful that one bean is enough to kill an adult.

Plant Record Breakers

- The giant bamboo can grow 90 cm (3 ft) in a day!
- The Pacific giant kelp has fronds 120 m (394 ft) long – that's taller than the Statue of Liberty!

- The leaves of the giant Amazonian water lily can grow to more than 2 m (6 ft) across!

- The tallest cactus in the world is the saguaro. A 250-year-old plant can be 20 m (65 ft) high and weigh 6 tonnes!
- Lotus seeds have been known to germinate more than 200 years after they were shed! Don't hold your breath!

FOOD FACTS

The food we eat today comes from many different parts of the world. Perhaps Sir Walter Raleigh set the trend when he discovered the potato in the New World and brought it back to England!

RICE BOWL

Rice has been a cultivated crop for at least 7,000 years. Today, more than half of the world's population eats it.

DAILY BREAD

The first bread was made more than 10,000 years ago. Nowadays, wheat fields in the major grain producing areas of the world are as vast as oceans.

MEAT

Cattle are bred mainly to provide meat and milk. They can be found all over the world, especially in India where there are nearly 300 million. Moooo!

Sheep are farmed for their wool and as meat. On the vast Australian sheep farms, a flock of 10,000 sheep may well wander an area of 400 sq km (150 sq miles), so the shepherds travel about on motor bikes!

A motorcycle round-up of Merino sheep in Australia. The Merino sheep is one of the world's great wool breeds.

THE WORLD'S SHOPPING BASKET

• In a year, the world eats 57,525,248 tonnes of tomatoes, 34,418,560 tonnes of cabbage and 40,597,200 tonnes of bananas!

• In Britain, 10 billion eggs are eaten annually.

• In India, many people are vegetarian, as Hindus believe all life is sacred, so they won't eat fish or meat.

STRANGE BUT TRUE

• The world's biggest ever cucumber weighed in at 9.1 kg (20 lb) – enough to make 1,137 cucumber sandwiches! Hungry?

• If all the grapes harvested in a year were collected together, they could bury Manhattan Island, New York 124 m (407 ft) down!

• In ancient China, fruit called lychees were considered to be so valuable that tax collectors would demand them as payment!

Hot, Hot, Hot!

About 12% of the Earth is covered by deserts and about another third is at risk from becoming desert land.

Top Three

The three largest deserts in the world are:

Sahara	8,600,000 sq km (3,320,000 sq miles)
Arabian	2,330,000 sq km (900,000 sq miles)
Gobi	1,200,000 sq km (463,000 sq miles)

Gobi desert

Carpet of Flowers

Deserts have less than 250 mm (10 in) of rain a year, and very few plants and animals are able to survive. Whenever it does rain, the entire desert comes alive with thousands of little flowers.

Desert plants are called 'ephemerals'. They have brightly coloured petals to attract the desert insects.

Dead Hot

If a person was stranded for a day in the Sahara desert with no water, no food and no shade, they would be dead by dusk. So remember to take a bottle of drink next time you're in the area!

Suit-able

Clothes for desert survival need to be long and loose and made of cotton. A cloth wrapped around the head with a gap for the eyes keeps the sand and wind out.

This Algerian man is wearing clothing to protect him from the severe heat.

Man-made Deserts

People have done much to actually help deserts develop. (Not very handy!) But they can reverse the process too.

Without hedges and trees, the wind blows all the topsoil away and crops are not so successful. Planting trees and other strong crops helps to stop the desert from taking over any more land.

This is a field of millet, planted on the edge of a sand dune in Niger.

SUBZERO!

Despite the fact that all fresh water in the Arctic and Antarctic is frozen solid, and the sea's surface is frozen, there's plenty of life at both ends of the Earth.

FROZEN SOLID

About 98% of the Antarctic is covered by a huge sheet of ice, over 4 km (2.5 miles) deep in places. Only a few mountain tops stick out.

Ice is so powerful that it can crush wooden ships, so special ships called *icebreakers* keep the navigation channels clear in the winter.

BELIEVE IT OR NOT...

The lowest temperature ever recorded in the world was at Vostok, Antarctica, in 1983. It was a nose-nipping, toe-curling -89°C (-128°F). That's seriously cold!

NO DIETING HERE!

Seals, walruses and whales have a special layer of fat under their skin called *blubber*, to keep out the cold.

This walrus could weigh as much as 1,600 kg (1.6 tons).

Seasonal Wear

The Arctic fox has two fur coats – one for summer and one for winter. The summer coat is brownish/grey and quite thin and short. The winter coat is snowy white, and the hairs are hollow inside to trap body warmth.

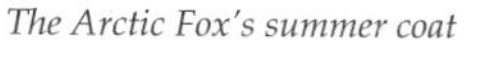

The Arctic Fox's summer coat

Antifreeze

Many Antarctic fish have antifreeze molecules in their bodies, so they can survive in the icy water.

The Arctic Fox's winter coat

Penguin chick and parent

Cuddling Up

Penguins are pretty good at keeping warm. Baby chicks stand on their parents' feet, huddled under a special pouch, until they are about 2 months old! Much warmer than snow and ice!

Cosy Coat

Long before the parka became fashionable, it was essential for survival in cold places! It was made from reindeer skin with the hide outside and the fur inside, for warmth. Mittens were sewn into the sleeves for extra protection.

HOUSE STYLE

People around the world live in all kinds of houses and homes – some in the country and some in cities.

Some people live in absolute luxury while others live in poverty, and often very close together.

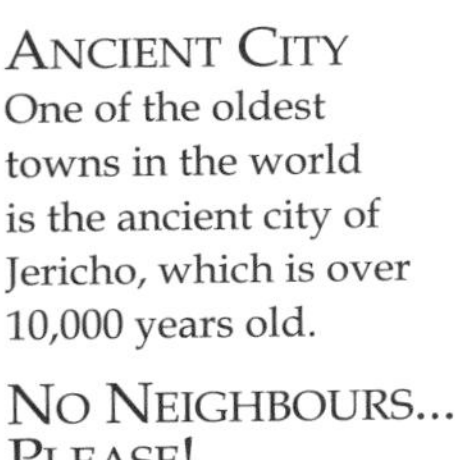

ANCIENT CITY

One of the oldest towns in the world is the ancient city of Jericho, which is over 10,000 years old.

NO NEIGHBOURS... PLEASE!

Some people will go to enormous lengths to be private! The palace shown here is perched on top of a rocky outcrop, so the owner could show everyone how important he was!

Summer Palace at Wadi Dahr, Yemen

Paper Walls

In Japan, houses were traditionally made of wood with sliding paper screens for doors and windows. It meant you had to be very careful with candles!

Snow House

During the hunting season, Inuits (Eskimos) built igloos as temporary bases. They were very cleverly designed to keep everyone warm and comfortable, and even had windows made with blocks of freshwater ice.

Houses in the Sky

Nowadays, land is so scarce in some places that all the buildings have to go up into the sky. Hong Kong and New York have very similar skylines.

Believe It or Not...

When the New York skyscrapers were erected, most of the construction work was done by Mohawk and Iroquois Indians who have no fear of heights.

People of The World

More tantalising world facts to impress your best friends or annoy your worst enemies!

Population

- One third of the world's people are under the age of 15.
- Three people are born every second, nearly 11,000 every hour and more than 255,000 every day.

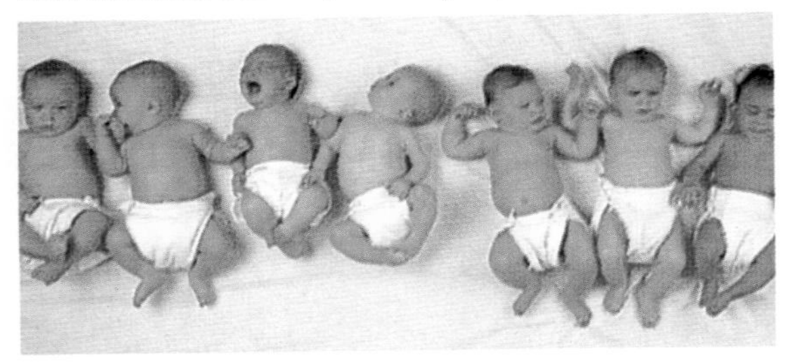

- There are 20 million refugees in the world – people who have fled their country in fear.

Cities

- Nearly 50% of the world's population, about 2.6 billion people, live in cities.
- The world's largest city is Tokyo, Japan, which has a total population of 25.77 million.

Richest

- The highest standard of living in the world is enjoyed by the Japanese.
- The world's three richest families, excluding Heads of State, all live in America.

Poorest

- The lowest standard of living in the world is in Guinea.
- One third of the developing world's children are under weight.
- Two thirds of the world's families do not have running water in their homes.
- Almost 80 million children in developing countries do not go to school.

Did You Know?

- 1,093 million people speak Mandarin Chinese. 420 million people speak English.
- Chicago International Airport in the USA is the busiest in the world – planes take off and land every 40 seconds!
- The largest gold reserves in the world are at Fort Knox, Kentucky, USA.

Fort Knox

EVERYONE IS DIFFERENT

Wherever you go in the world, all human society is based on the family. However, everyone is different and customs can vary considerably from country to country.

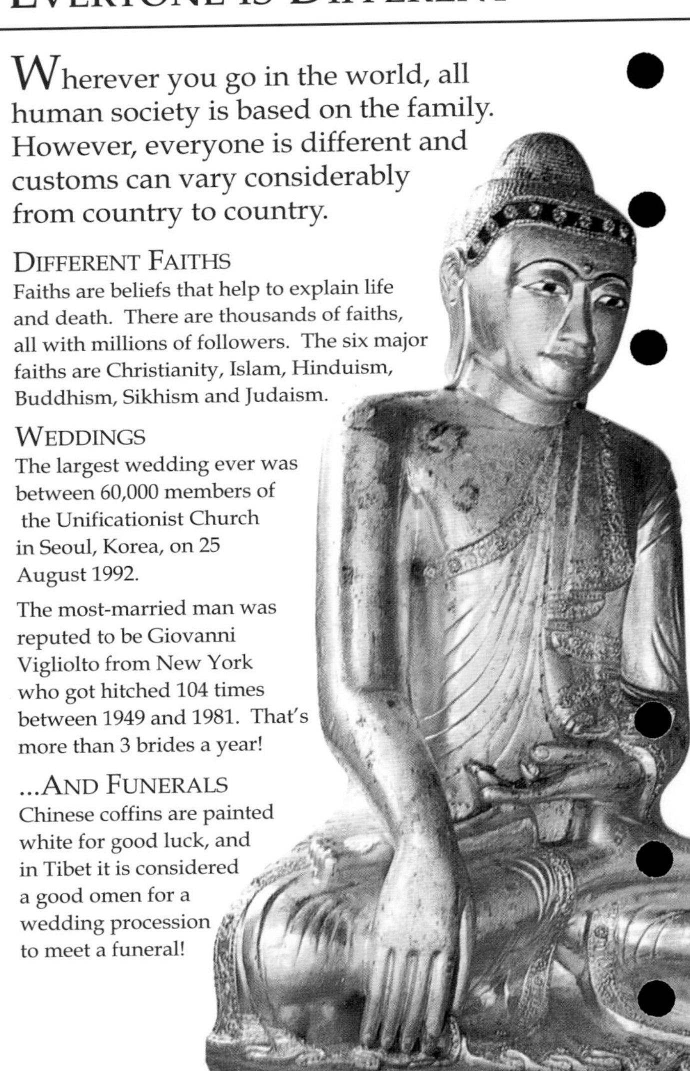

DIFFERENT FAITHS

Faiths are beliefs that help to explain life and death. There are thousands of faiths, all with millions of followers. The six major faiths are Christianity, Islam, Hinduism, Buddhism, Sikhism and Judaism.

WEDDINGS

The largest wedding ever was between 60,000 members of the Unificationist Church in Seoul, Korea, on 25 August 1992.

The most-married man was reputed to be Giovanni Vigliolto from New York who got hitched 104 times between 1949 and 1981. That's more than 3 brides a year!

...AND FUNERALS

Chinese coffins are painted white for good luck, and in Tibet it is considered a good omen for a wedding procession to meet a funeral!

Celebrations

In China, the Dragon Boat Festival is held to give thanks for food and water.

Thanksgiving Day, in the USA, is a traditional family meal of turkey and pumpkin pie, to celebrate the harvest.

Divali, in India, celebrates the harvest with decorative lights and offerings to Lakshmi, the Hindu goddess of wealth.

The carnival in Venice celebrates the end of Lent, the Christian period of denial.

Dreamtime

The Aborigines in Australia believe that their ancestors created the world and everything in it. These ancestors can be human, animal or plant, and the creation time is called Dreamtime.

Crisis!

Little by little, humans are damaging and destroying the world we live in. Here are some of the things we get up to.

Wasting Natural Resources

It takes half a million trees to supply Americans with their Sunday newspapers every week!

The richest 20% of the world's population uses 75% of the world's metals, 85% of its wood and 60% of its food – and most of it ends up on rubbish tips.

Smog

The city of Los Angeles, USA, uses 33 million litres of petrol, diesel and aviation fuel a day, producing more than 12,000 tonnes of atmospheric pollution every 24 hours.

Fox scavenging amongst litter left by humans

Animal Dustbins

Rubbish dumped thoughtlessly can poison or seriously injure animals in the wild.

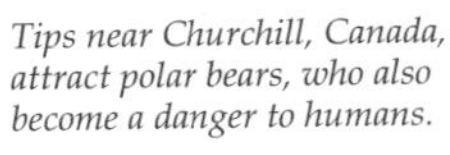

Tips near Churchill, Canada, attract polar bears, who also become a danger to humans.

Acid Rain

Acid rain is formed by two gases which are pumped into the atmosphere by factories and cars. When the gases mix with water, they make tiny drops of acid which falls as rain, damaging plants and wildlife.

Grubby Moths

The peppered moth has gradually become darker and darker to be better camouflaged against sooty tree trunks.

How You Can Help

YOU can help save the Earth's resources. Try to:

- Recycle bottles, glass, cans and paper
- Switch off lights when not in use
- Walk, cycle or use the bus instead of a car

INDEX

Acknowledgements: Museo Archeologico di Napoli; Natural History Museum; Science Museum, London.

Picture Credits: (KEY: a=above, b=bottom/below, c=centre, l=left, r=right, t=top) Adams Picture Library: 41; Bryan & Cherry Alexander: 38t; 46cl; Alison Anholt-White: Back cover br; 28br; Heather Angel/Biofotos: 31t; British Antarctic Survey: Back cover bc; 7; Bruce Colman Ltd: 28cra;/Jane Burton: 46br;/MPL Fogden: 36b;/Kim Taylor: 47b;/Norman Tomalin: 42b; Michael Copsey: 21; B Cosgrove: 28clb; James Davis Travel Photography: Front cover br; European Space Agency: 27cla; Robert Harding Picture Library: 6bl; 6br; 22br; 25b; 37t;/GA Mather: 31b; Hutchison/Stephen Pern: 43t; The Image Bank/Steve Bronstein: 15b;/Gary Calle: 1; 25t;/Don & Liysa King: 16; 39;/Michael Salas: 45b; Frank Lane Picture Agency/ S. Jonasson: 10;/Silvestris: 47t; Magnum Photos/Steve McCurry: 37b; NASA: 2b; 5; 15t; National Centre for Atmospheric Research: 27cr; Oxford Scientific Films/Doug Allen: 39br;/John Downer: 9br;/Kim Westerkov: 22bl; Pictor International: 14; 44; RK Pilsbury: 26cr; 26tr; 28cla; Popperfoto: 12; Royal Botanic Gardens, Kew: 33cl; Science Photo Library: 19; 29tc; 29tr;/Claude Nuridsany & Marie Perennon: Front Cover tl; 29tl;/ESA: Front cover c;/Keith Kent: 3;/Tom van Sant/Geosphere Project, Santa Monica: 4b; Clive Streeter: 36t; Tony Stone Images/Tony Craddock: 18;/Stephen Studd: 34c;/Stuart Westmorland: 17t; Sygma: 24; Trip/Helene Rogers: 40; Zefa Pictures: 23; 30; 42t;/APL: 34bl;/Resea 43b.

Additional Photography: Geoff Brightling, Jane Burton, Gordon Clayton, Michael Dunning, Andreas von Einsiedel, Steve Gorton, Frank Greenaway, Nick Hall, Colin Keates, Andrew McRobb, Karl Shone, James Stevenson, Kim Taylor, Jerry Young.

Use the Earth sticker on the fold-out Time Line in your Funfax Eyewitness Library. *See inside cover for details.*